A Revolutionary Calendar

PREVIOUS PUBLICATIONS BY ZOË SKOULDING

The Celestial Set-Up (Oystercatcher, 2020)
Footnotes to Water (Seren, 2019)
Teint (Hafan Books, 2016)
The Museum of Disappearing Sounds (Seren, 2013)
Remains of a Future City (Seren, 2008)
From Here [with Simonetta Moro] (Dusie, 2008)
Dark Wires [with Ian Davidson] (West House Books, 2007)
The Mirror Trade (Seren, 2004)
Tide Table (Gwasg Pantycelyn, 1998)

Zoë Skoulding

A
Revolutionary
Calendar

Shearsman Books

First published in the United Kingdom in 2020 by
Shearsman Books Ltd
PO Box 4239
Swindon
SN3 9FN

Shearsman Books Ltd Registered Office
30–31 St. James Place, Mangotsfield, Bristol BS16 9JB
(this address not for correspondence)

www.shearsman.com

ISBN 978-1-84861-690-5

Acknowledgments

This project owes its beginnings to a residency at Les Récollets in Paris in
2014, hosted by the Mairie de Paris and the Institut Français. 'Germinal' was
published in *Wired to the Dynamo: Poetry & prose in honour of John Barnie*,
edited by Matt Jarvis (Cinnamon Press, 2018). It was also exhibited as a series
of prints in *Unus Multorum* at Plas Bodfa in 2020. An extract from 'Prairial'
was published in *Wretched Strangers*, edited by Ágnes Lehóczky and J.T. Welsch
(Boiler House Press, 2018). 'Frimaire' was published as 2018's secular
non-advent calendar from Crater Press, in collaboration with the artist
Sharon Kivland. Other extracts have appeared in *Molly Bloom, Datableed,
Paris Lit Up, Gorse, Erotoplasty, Tentacular, Reliquiae* and *PN Review*.
Many thanks to all the editors.

CONTENTS

Vendémiaire

1. *Raisin* GRAPE

the city trickles down your throat in blood
swallowed days swallow you crushed
you leave your trace in the season mutating

what state is not
a state of change stand up

2. *Safran* SAFFRON

crushed yellow stains
your fingers from stamen
to sunset to gold

in this struggle the trace of
a head or a planet turning

3. *Châtaigne* CHESTNUT

after the summer comes a glut
of chestnuts blackened in fire
erupting a shell cracks

between thumb and finger
if it looks like a brain eat it

4. *Colchique* AUTUMN CROCUS

a crack in the bulb a clean start
and late green light spring on repeat
goes naked and leafless

round and round and
falling into storms we hold together

5. *Cheval* HORSE

there came a white horse
not that old story
but a break in the surface

        where the edge of a wave
repeats nothing

6. *Balsamine* TOUCH-ME-NOT BALSAM

scatter wide in the insurgency
quick in the hand
a seedpod

        explodes nothingness
in the human system of a garden

7. *Carotte* CARROT

scrape earth from skin
where bright sugar
seeps through that other

        taste of what's come up
from underneath

8. *Amaranthe* AMARANTH

this red means nothing
if you've forgotten hunger
a handful of seeds spitting in the pan

        after all the burnings
where love lies bleeding

9. *Panais* PARSNIP

at root is an idea you can't know
in the dark only taste is it sweet
how do you tell

              what should have been buried
and what must keep pushing back

10. *Cuve* VAT

while tomorrow's wine is sleeping
tap out yesterday's rhythm
that tomorrow no longer believes

          in which every tomorrow
is better than today

11. *Pomme de terre* POTATO

scrabble under the skin of earth
for the starch pearl mud apple and ask

         what future lies under the skin
of the seasons you can still decipher
or the darknesses you can still count

12. *Immortelle* STRAWFLOWER

you can still shine yellow
dry to a papery thinness

         not the flower but the dead
shape of its idea still gleaming
indestructible

13. *Potiron* SQUASH

a gouged out gourd a sunset
what were you dreaming of

      coming and going a movement
accomplished at sixes and sevens
return sunrise

14. *Réséda* MIGNONETTE

belief in sky is what holds it up
roots hidden in sun

      only heady scent escapes
the fight between yellows
in these ragged petals

15. *Âne* DONKEY

ears tuned forwards a pull on a back hoof
a footing lost and found

      always change
moving through fur and lashes
a smoking muzzle

16. *Belle de nuit* MARVEL OF PERU

who has your attention and what's it worth
in the stretched-out hours

      she comes in colours
steps into night's movement
glittering where darkness grows by one

17. *Citrouille* PUMPKIN

time to turn into another
sunset globe hold steady

       after all what do I know about
where this carriage is heading
with its windows all on fire

18. *Sarrasin* BUCKWHEAT

even grain doesn't escape
otherness a dark seed

       time doesn't come
as if arriving from somewhere else
you move and it's what you are

19. *Tournesol* SUNFLOWER

roll a ring of flame against the sky
as earth turns on a point of light

       this uncertain hope
takes more than one
blazing head

20. *Pressoir* WINEPRESS

that was god's blood then printers' ink
pressed down in the word made flesh

       more blood in the economy
won't save anyone
it's time for leverage

21. *Chanvre* HEMP

laid out in dew where colonies of mould

       advance in flecks on steel-grey fibre
cleaning and brightening
this work of loss not us
a rope against the troubles

22. *Pêche* PEACH

the day you're dreaming of is already here

       a bloom of down settles on the news
as chlorophyll degrades and love
costs nothing as it ripens
a darker pigmentation coming through

23. *Navet* TURNIP

in place of a planet

       turning purple
red or greenish glazed
she remembered turnips
the room grew smaller

24. *Amarillis* AMARYLLIS

what's the point of shepherding

       lost names Amaryllis
a tangle in the air
all bitterness and glitter
gaudy bloom

25. *Boeuf* STEER

lurches at the grid

      a flank scored into
cuts of gendered meat he doesn't know
his weight shifts tremulous
in grass and muscle hot breath

26. *Aubergine* AUBERGINE

yes but can you read what it says

      not the pale flesh
tracing round the seed like faint letters
but the tissues of knowledge
not your own

27. *Piment* CHILI PEPPER

who or what inflicts it

      pain is red
is too simple a diagnosis
for the edge of feeling you can't reach
between kiss and pepper spray

28. *Tomate* TOMATO

translation ripples a supply chain

      from wolf peach to golden apple
water grows fat on capital
I say truncation of ACC synthase
you say endless summer

29. *Orge* BARLEY

a head thinking inflorescence

      a scarecrow marks a human
boundary roughed up
in wind where birds loop
in spikes and fractals

30. *Tonneau* BARREL

lignin breakdown to vanilla

      oak in the mouth where woods
are the shape of waiting
in seepage of oxygen this red darkens
the trees speak with your tongue

Brumaire

1. *Pomme* APPLE

what comes round again what
breaks? as a sphere goes out of
sync   we turn into another season
time   breathing in a change of skins
these apples mottled russet

2. *Céleri* CELERY

how far down will you go? a knotted
root curls back on an old struggle
          which is to say forward
where this invisible line of force
pushes out through hearts and ribs

3. *Poire* PEAR

is this weight in the hand a balance
of tree against ground against
acetone sky?   gold fogs
the human violence of hours
in every drop of unseen sun

4. *Betterave* BEETROOT

how does this darkness taste to you?
under the mist there are so many
ways to interrogate earth
          scrub off the mud then tell me
what interred red bleeds from it

5. *Oie* GOOSE

is it time yet to go back to the assembly line
of golden eggs? oscillations
in a phase relationship of light
and inner calibration   time to
throw off these heavy feathers

6. *Héliotrope* EUROPEAN TURNSOLE

if it's day that's moving where is now?
even these petals in a cupboard
turn to the sun and fold at night
        false dawn starts earlier every
day which is anything but clear as

7. *Figue* FIG

what's that hidden in the leaves?
your hand's a *mano fico* warding off
the eye that stares all night insomniac
                drowsing flowers
curled inside false fruit

8. *Scorsonère* BLACK SALSIFY

how did we sleep so long? the question
is a curved line running through
release of hormones body temperature
rhythmical lapping of events   the breaking
news   a black root's milky sap

9. *Alisier* WILD SERVICE TREE

what did you search for in your sleep?
fingers and tongues come alive
        in lost outlines of names
sweet gritty berries   chequerboard   bark
it's time to wake up   nothing to see here

10. *Charrue* PLOUGH

if a revolution is a turning year what
changes in these daily rotations?
furrowed ground   furrowed brow
the scored field beyond the grasp
of the hand on tangled lines

11. *Salsifis* SALSIFY

this was what we were promised
wasn't it? oh look   they've vanished
not oysters but oyster plant
there's enough but it isn't   can't get no
they still want the pageant the cruel glamour

12. *Macre* WATER CHESTNUT

if everything's in flux then why
are you standing still? the stream's
in chill delay   but that's a lie
floating on the surface
pulling on slender jointed roots

13. *Topinambour* Jerusalem Artichoke

what route was ever not foreign?
we're going round in circles   again
        Brazil to *girasole* Jerusalem
sun travels underground heads turn
at a likeness   neither earth nor apple

14. *Endive* Endive

how can you still tell which way's up?
        a body moves around
another causing different seasons
as pale leaves turn on their axis
hidden from the mean fictitious sun

15. *Dindon* Turkey

what did we vote for anyway?
                nothing as exotic
as a fleshy wattle a shake of the feathers
gobbling snouts dropped
in the noise of a democratic system

16. *Chervi* Skirret

is it hunger or hope that pushes through?
        in the scrabble for skinny roots
fingers and bones dig down in x-ray
delicate survival sugared into light
        work towards it with whatever

17. *Cresson* WATERCRESS

what makes one dark differ from another?
on the stream bed pepper leaf
       ties itself in knots
unstoppable water moving through it
like a pattern of thought or weather

18. *Dentelaire* LEADWORT

well this time is it tragedy or farce?
the slow music of the calendar is
phrase beyond fog   fog beyond
content   or the ghost of a fog
happening all over again

19. *Grenade* POMEGRANATE

is that why you went away? everything
       begins before it begins
a luminous red globe unpeeled from bitter skin
go deeper   every minute indented
       bleeding to its own seed

20. *Herse* HARROW

what's the word for this? suddenly
awake again   needles and hands
clocking the repetition   breaking up
and smoothing out the surface as I try to hold
my balance on this one remaining clod of earth

21. *Bacchante* BUSH GROUNDSEL

could anything be more empty than your updates?
I can't establish distance from my own hand   let alone
today's catastrophe or viscous weather
sticking to my story   let's haze over
the soft invasion   of fruiting clouds

22. *Azerole* CRETE HAWTHORN

how long can you stare at this name
flaming in passage?   *az-zou'rour*
as the sun roars round   from one land
to another   berries rust red to scarlet
vermilion orpiment chrome yellow gold

23. *Garance* MADDER

there was something I had to do today
but what? long and narrow leaves
stand like a star where silence
punctuates the days   breath rises   held
suffused in pinkish red   unanswered

24. *Orange* ORANGE

who are you really in love with?
                          how terrible
the condition that distinguishes
animals and plants from inorganic matter
skin of bright oils   your teeth in its pith

25. *Faisan* PHEASANT

can you see this?   the future struts
and chatters into flight   behind you
tail feathers   spangle in a landscape
where contours soften into cloud
breakthrough   falling

26. *Pistache* PISTACHIO

what new green is hidden
            where the old green cracks?
in the bleached shell at the edge of sleep
light cuts through this planetary
circling   we've all been here before

27. *Macjonc* SWEETPEA

not an exact image? exactly
an image of a flower   unfolding
its scent in another season
creased across a palm   where time's
a cloud arising from events

28. *Coing* QUINCE

            what were we thinking?
those days   before our minds
were made of winter's sudden onset
wax flesh blushed in syrup
lit up   by a low red sun

29. *Cormier* SERVICE TREE

if you can't name it are you sure that it exists?
branches in mist are a skeleton code
connecting sense to   shifting
information   say ash or bitter golden
apple   while the blank sky locks down

30. *Rouleau* ROLLER

is this a line or a moving volume
that even calendars can't flatten?
             white sheets   a field in fog
beyond my fingertips horizons crumple
a day that touches   that I can almost touch

Frimaire

1. *Raiponce* RAMPION

the sentence braided
together in the
falling staircase of
winter never ends;
there's a connection;

2. *Turnep* FLAT TURNIP

someone's winking;
a planet spins off
an unhinged axis
another day still here;
a blurred head turns;

3. *Chicorée* CHICORY

so you wake up and
smell this sky; a blue
star opens in a clock-
work movement a learnt
taste for bitterness;

4. *Nèfle* MEDLAR

this bletted mush
scooped out of night
is a mouthful of
seeds; what starts in
sleep won't end there;

5. *Cochon* Pig

there is no poison
in the pig
down to its trotters;
that taste of death
is already inside you;

6. *Mâche* Lamb's Lettuce

from rat's ear to hen's
grass comes water
sucked into leaf;
a lamb's tongue is
blood and chlorophyll;

7. *Chou-fleur* Cauliflower

fat replicas of trees
breed solid cloud;
fractal belonging
flowers in the slow
division of a thought;

8. *Miel* Honey

here's an imagined
structure of sweetness;
whose algorithm
is it humming
under your breath;

9. *Genièvre* JUNIPER

in front of itself or
slightly behind
a branch thickens; fire
comes without smoke
smoke without scent;

10. *Pioche* PICK

break it up; don't
break it up; this is
the pointed edge of
force that punctuates
a day scored through;

11. *Cire* WAX

all that bee work
wasn't for this blue light;
in a dot and flicker
another hour's gone
no strut now no fret;

12. *Raifort* HORSERADISH

eyes water in such
rough heat that the day
blinks; as recoil is
also craving what you
recall will happen;

13. *Cèdre* CEDAR

the scent of a box
opens on the forest in
your limbs; it branches
through today's
low sun citrine buzz;

14. *Sapin* FIR

we come to our senses
in the needling under-
foot a skin of resins;
this force to which we
come among forces;

15. *Chevreuil* ROE DEER

a wild arc of muscle
wheels away from
premonition; blood
halts for a moment
in fingers and screens;

16. *Ajonc* GORSE

why pretend you're
not thinking of kisses
as a sudden yellow;
lips and flowers
quiver into swarms;

17. *Cyprès* Cypress

a cut stump doesn't
always regrow but
stays cut; another
borrowed day
starts in its shadow;

18. *Lierre* Ivy

if it winds round is
glued enough but
also growing thought
becomes stone as stone
thought; a surface locks;

19. *Sabine* Savin

a blue forest grows
in the blood where
it would run again;
a body hinges on
an altered moon;

20. *Hoyau* Axe

a blade swings
against spilt wood;
warm twice over in
the work the split
falls between;

21. *Érable sucre* SILVER MAPLE

bark crackles in
mosaic a rough
glaze; under the
frozen surface
comes this force;

22. *Bruyère* HEATHER

don't try to count
what adds up to
this slippage of
colour; another
sky bleeds through;

23. *Roseau* REED

thinking grass
bends into a
hollow music;
what doesn't break
grows louder;

24. *Oseille* SORREL

and what breaks
where the words
won't go grows
brighter; a sharp
green hums;

25. *Grillon* CRICKET

the singer of that
song is already
dead; below ground
a scratched record
a waiting egg;

26. *Pignon* PINE NUT

day's arrival haunts
its own shape;
inside a double
shell slow growth
turns and breaks;

27. *Liège* CORK OAK

stopped bottles can't
hold a sudden push
fermenting;
pockets of air
resist and spring;

28. *Truffe* TRUFFLE

value glows all
over the relation
at root a snuffling
underground;
catch this scent;

29. *Olive* OLIVE

oil pressed from
dark fruit won't
hold summer's
shape; what runs
runs out; days ooze;

30. *Pelle* SHOVEL

when push comes to
love your future is
the skin of the past;
the sentence is
broken like this;

Nivôse

1. *Tourbe* PEAT

bogged down in what you might need to know
for tomorrow but don't at least not yet
you toast the coming day in phenols
soak up the flood as life under pressure
...
grass moss lichen mice roots human compacted

2. *Houille* COAL

and sink further under where there's no-one
to draw a line no line to draw and start again
...
the slow burn of being human a crushed
layer in futures undermined
right there behind your back don't look

3. *Bitume* ASPHALT

in this collusion of rock and algae across millennia
never forget how to walk on hell a forward pitch
...
as every human road
unfolds a blackness
gaze at flowers

4. *Soufre* SULPHUR

let's say brimstone or everlasting primrose path
...
strike a light in the event and
time flares out
so neither can I not think of
this as sad exploding human yellow

5. *Chien* DOG

a human dog marks the spot
…
he writes his own needs with his teeth
in everything and his day
runs in circles wagging
revolution by its tail

6. *Lave* LAVA

so earth is suddenly effusive outpour
from a human fullness approaching
only to diminish then
in scattered flecks of ash
…
had we but world enough

7. *Terre végétale* HUMUS

after having been or before living
earth settles into what crops up
the root of the problem persisting
from human to hubris to this
…
mud stuck under a fingernail

8. *Fumier* MANURE

well it must be national
shite day coming round again
…
I woke up travelling through
the inside of a horse
yesterday's grass outrunning human sadness

9. *Salpêtre* SALTPETRE

if human time is speed of decay
fear of hunger bacteria moving into meat
a crust of salts draws water
as minerals bubble through a wall
…
a shelter crumbles

10. *Fléau* FLAIL

a human movement lashing out at a
balance between two sides unsteadily
sifting grain from husk the living daylights
from the darkened mass
…
or floundering from failing

11. *Granit* GRANITE

a bubbling up of lava settles and
cools below ground or
seeps into biography
…
here we are at rock bottom a slab
and a hand chiselling a human span

12. *Argile* CLAY

silt-scented pale in the hand
pinched into a figure with its gloopy
excess smoothed over
…
this human stickiness
makes even mud a vessel for itself

13. *Ardoise* SLATE

the splintering wall cleaves to itself
or shatters into cloud falling
through the valley the dropped rock
echoes through a rasp of human breath
…
a hand erasing letters or dust or letters or dust

14. *Grès* SANDSTONE

time falls through human hands becomes
a glass becomes the hand turning on a face
becomes the sediment becomes
compacted rock weathered
…
the wind wears it down and water

15. *Lapin* RABBIT

in the disappearance of white flashes of tail
grey streaks into grass
as movement replaces origin
…
a human carries a word left dangling
from an empty hand

16. *Silex* FLINT

sometimes cuts itself falls apart and
breaks without a hand to chip its edges
…
what came first sharp instrument
or human sparks rocks intentions wars
arrowheads fired into the present

17. *Marne* MARLSTONE

…
in this unstable composition
a human slipping under rain
I came together for a lifetime but whose
silt am I carrying give me
your hand at the bottom of the lake

18. *Pierre à chaux* LIMESTONE

everything that comes out white
caves in
a human emptiness the dark
skeletal fragments coral molluscs
…
façades hold up hand-cut

19. *Marbre* MARBLE

this gleaming is the ratio of life to what's thrown out of it
fail again fail with complete success
…
you have to find the knot
a hand untied or contradiction in forces
to make a human figure emerge

20. *Van* WINNOWING BASKET

in the game of lightness and
weight this human load of
words thrown up in wind
flies like a whole basket of indicators
or slips through the hand as chaff
…

21. *Pierre à plâtre* GYPSUM

plastered again in layers
repeating the surface
…
between the eye and the angle the steady hand
a desert rose blooms in the expanse
of walls crumbling into rock

22. *Sel* SALT

more than a pinch in the hand
I love you blooms in the long march
who owns the sea's time
a troublesome question
…
evaporation of a changing state

23. *Fer* IRON

a velvet hand in a velvet industrial
pocket when revolution turns in
cogs of thinking money
…
air reddens to the taste of blood
on the edge of the lung

24. *Cuivre* COPPER

this bright trace in blood liver muscle bone
if you lost it you'd hardly know
a handful of pennies down the back of a chair
what change unloosed
…
what verdigris weathering

25. *Chat* CAT

in a claw extended and retracted
a day extends to long stretch
…
unbounded pleasure or cyclic agitation
a movement curls around a hand
shifting mass and density

26. *Étain* TIN

miners' hands stained with arsenic
pastry rolled up at the edges
a sure grip on survival the day's fuel
…
beans or peaches
it is what it says on it

27. *Plomb* LEAD

a bad dream bright silver with
a shade of blue comes to the surface
…
and hands you a straight
line to the bottom pencilled in
the details rubbed off the calendar

28. *Zinc* ZINC

when the mineral trace of poetry is gone
look out for the signs such as
…
poor neurological function
weak immunity diarrhoea allergies thinning hair
leaky gut and rashes a shaking hand

29. *Mercure* MERCURY

a level rising underneath
…
a raised hand the flickering
of pressure in the blood
threaded through by language
in a slow blink that was a life

30. *Crible* SIEVE

the weave of it
…
the shake-up to an edge
caught in the hand with fingers reaching
far into sleep where years falling out of
line come sifted through like snow

Pluviôse

1. *Lauréole* SPURGE-LAUREL

: here's a day where
everything that isn't water
must be time that rests
on dry bones
listening and waiting

2. *Mousse* MOSS

so to a condensation:
here's a ceiling of moss
glowing over skulls
what's revolution if not
where what goes around comes

3. *Fragon* BUTCHER'S BROOM

clean sweep: here's
a new second
a second
gone in the hours
and their uncut edges

4. *Perce-neige* SNOWDROP

petals don't shelter
but pierce: here's
your skyline my skin
across the frame
interrupted by a blink

5. *Taureau* BULL

across the horizon
a cut-out gap in the sky
where this language was:
here's the rain's
missing punctuation

6. *Laurier-thym* LAURUSTINUS

when time's restitched
you clock the surface
its needles and hands: here
the present's
an embroidery

7. *Amadouvier* TINDER POLYPORE

kindling grows from
bark: here's the flash
after the event fixed
by the stop I watch
myself making

8. *Mézéréon* DAPHNE MEZEREUM

a pause between
double lives scored
into tree trunk:
here's dead skin
grafted on to sap

9. *Peuplier* POPLAR

: here's your stand-off
striping the rain
in exclamation
willow won't you
come closer

10. *Coignée* AXE

felled at the root:
here's an endpoint
sharpened by split
wood scented
with beginning

11. *Ellébore* HELLEBORE

stink of green bells in the dripping leaves
obviously I'm your poison: here's
the small hell of a missed
connection mis-
translation

12. *Brocoli* BROCCOLI

perception of bitterness
varies depending on taste
receptors on the tongue: here's
a forest in my mouth
I'm clearing it to say this

13. *Laurier* LAUREL

wreathed in green:
here's a shadow fact
advancing on the day
a cat hidden
in the leaves a lie

14. *Avelinier* FILBERT

the cracked nut furred
on the tongue as yet
no more than the thought
of a flower: here's a hiss of sap
waking in the wood

15. *Vache* COW

another day another rumination:
here's a chance to chew it over
yesterday's grass a hardly digestible fact
moving through the upward
curve of spring

16. *Buis* BOX TREE

formed by squares of hedges
neoclassical design a soft wind
through the orderly grid an arbour
with a fountain at the centre: here's
a calendar as boxing in of spring

17. *Lichen* LICHEN

a planetary bloom runs rings round
history books living on thin air in long
exposures of rock glaciers cliffs tundra
the years radiate: here's what happened
in case you missed it

18. *If* YEW

shadow bites day to this black-out
we never saw coming
call it a wound breaking the continuum
but is it yours or mine oozing
stickily: here's the biggest if

19. *Pulmonaire* LUNGWORT

it was your breath that slowed
a hope for tomorrow running ahead
down the station steps:
here's another language
hidden in a lung

20. *Serpette* BILLHOOK

: here the eye cuts from the distance
to what's at hand a curved blade
slicing back exterior time
tangled in the undergrowth
that won't stay down

21. *Thlaspi* PENNYCRESS

winter stops everything
happening at once
as oil swells inside a seed:
here's a crushed season to fuel
the engines crashing into spring

22. *Thimelé* ROSE DAPHNE

it hasn't happened yet but when it does
what scent breaks daily geometry:
here's suspense in the toxic leaves
lanceolate evergreen a bright head
bursting a line that doesn't exist

23. *Chiendent* COUCH GRASS

the dog chews grass and
grass tightens its grip
running under a system
wanting rid: here's
a remedy repeating

24. *Traînasse* KNOTWEED

all tied up in flow charts
every route a catastrophe
every step another knot:
here's a solution write a line
and then cast out another

25. *Lièvre* HARE

or leap into tomorrow: here's
a circle of muscle uncoiling
from the haunch these long hind legs
the chief organs of motion
are most effective when moving uphill

26. *Guède* WOAD

boil it to the brilliant hue
of double-coded nationhood
tramp up Snowdon with our woad on
faces painted blue: here the ground
is starred with yellow flowers

27. *Noisetier* HAZEL

tie it in a knot it doesn't break
or wave it as a wand undo what's done
do something else: here catkins
burst in firework formation
going on and on in the rain

28. *Cyclamen* SOWBREAD

how much of love or anything's endurance
you'll know about that if you're
still here: the same poem
the same kiss the same arrival
or red hot petal excess

29. *Chélidoine* CELANDINE

is good to sharpen the sight for it
cleanseth and consumeth away slimie things
that cleave about the ball of the eye:
here's where you weren't paying attention
look harder at this yellow blinking back

30. *Traineau* SLEIGH

what you draw what you drag across
late snow melting in drizzle or pull
across the ice is a day's weight: here's
all you need from yesterday sliding
from the other side of the still-frozen lake

Ventôse

1. *Tussilage* COLTSFOOT

because these atoms came from stars
all that holds them is a breath –
a fringed yellow sun turning
over the unwashed dishes – you're here
then everywhere

2. *Cornouiller* DOGWOOD

after the ice has gone and the snow
the only colour is this mass
of flaming branches – dagger lines
through clogged woods where
old tomorrows are still smouldering

3. *Violier* STOCK

what flowers isn't linear but loops back
in time and weather – instant petals furl –
what I just said won't snap off into
anyone's history – that's you already
catching the scent of spring's non-arrival

4. *Troène* PRIVET

take this clipped-back green where the berries
come and the birds – a private edge –
take ambiguous poisons of ownership –
take this decocted bark against
the trouble of elsewhere

5. *Bouc* BILLY GOAT

at the centre of his own weathertime –
since the revolution is what revolves
round him – he's tethered to the sky – all of it
sweeping round on the tip of his horns –
all of it full of his very own stench

6. *Asaret* WILD GINGER

leaves crowd in multiple curled hearts –
pages where the same old story
grows again – unreadable as the scent
of what it isn't exactly – never was –
but if you shut your eyes and breathe in –

7. *Alaterne* ITALIAN BUCKTHORN

green on paler green on cream – each leaf
a laying of maps – transparencies
of changing coastlines shifts
in population or the patchy spread of
weather – here and now heavier

8. *Violette* VIOLET

making an early appearance
a fragile nod to sugar and soap –
the violence of light
splits your head
against a blue wind

9. *Marceau* GOAT WILLOW

there should be more goats
in the willows – more
goats waywardly clambering –
more willows disappearing
behind yellowish goat teeth

10. *Bêche* SPADE

call a spade a monument
to hands – a handle framing sky
a blade locked into earth
upright on the horizon –
if you dare – dare now –

11. *Narcisse* NARCISSUS

you're all ears to the echo
of your own voice sounding
in its loneliness – a blaze of
golden rhetoric and nobody
nobody there –

12. *Orme* ELM

what passes and stands
still on the skyline –
skeleton structure of a myth
branches into cloud
lines about to fall

13. *Fumeterre*   COMMON FUMITORY

oh just a smoking earth
tears in your eyes – the usual
mess blurring the edges
between cause and effect –
but watch this space –

14. *Vélar*   HEDGE MUSTARD

look what gets thrown up
in the shattered ground –
a wiry tangled stem and yellow
petals – you could almost believe
that every poison has this antidote

15. *Chèvre*   NANNY GOAT

bleat is a broken question
pushed into forbidden leaves
a flexed lip browsing –
the heaviness of milk
against sprung muscle

16. *Épinard*   SPINACH

first green flickers against
the mineral darkness –
cut and come again –
a theory of resistance
still holding water

17. *Doronic* LEOPARD'S BANE

daisy wheel of sun on bitter grey
where there's no stopping
on the yellow lines or anywhere –
leaves furl out to their margins
irregular and toothed

18. *Mouron* SCARLET PIMPERNEL

when all planned outcomes are in disarray
just pretend to be pretending
not to know anything – those elusive petals
falling on your shoulders are still
someone else's blood not freedom

19. *Cerfeuil* CHERVIL

laced with desire and pushed up
in fronds of green – give it
the chop and swirl – an undertone
of aniseed a taste of happiness –
oh no that's not enough

20. *Cordeau* TWINE

the strength of a plural snaps tight –
I've got no freedom without yours
in the numbers game
that holds it all together
in a three-stranded twist

21. *Mandragore* MANDRAKE

to keep it dead – whatever you just
dug up – soak it in the milk
in which you drowned three bats
dry it in verbena and wrap it in a shroud –
but if it's the root of your scream – scream now

22. *Persil* PARSLEY

the mouth is rocks and peril
where a tongue stumbles –
read garnish as warning –
whiteness washes over bleached
ground where nothing grows

23. *Cochléaria* SCURVY GRASS

returning from the voyage it's
a hunger for green that sets off
searching – the taste
of elsewhere flowers
at your feet in salt and tar

24. *Pâquerette* DAISY

love me love me not you never
leave the whole year round
I crush you pull your petals
one by one at night you
only blink – days pass

25. *Thon* TUNA

in a rush of blue night passes
days come to the surface
as predator or prey – go home
and restart the cycle
but get it right this time

26. *Pissenlit* DANDELION

the lions have all but disappeared
with their yellow teeth – counting
hours or down to death is so much
pissing in the wind – what to do but wish
on thin air for a day already gone

27. *Sylve* FOREST

green turns over silver where hidden
ears shade echoes of survival – how far
could you run now without
touching the ground – to what
beginning could you possibly return

28. *Capillaire* MAIDENHAIR FERN

tomorrow's hanging by a thin
black line – waterfall-delicate
too much or not enough
sun or drainage – all this
wavering on the brink

29. *Frêne* ASH

fissured bark looks old – does it
sound as old as poetry
or the greying remnants of a fire
where helicopter seeds
are circling to the rescue

30. *Plantoir* DIBBER

hit me with your dibber stick – a little
spring rhythm in the broken ground
where what comes up is nothing
but a mirage of stockpiled rations
and longed-for disaster

Germinal

1. *Primevère* PRIMROSE

first yellow yes
but the very first
rose of the first
spring firsting
(a honeyed fist)

2. *Platane* PLANE

bark peels off in patches
leaving a mottled trunk
(inside spring pushes
out new skins) or
thickens and cracks

3. *Asperge* ASPARAGUS

sparrow grass marks you
greenscented
leaving its tang in your water
all this hurry into life
(a lily stem)

4. *Tulipe* TULIP

still life never
motionless but fragile
in wind a turban
unwound (how
far a flower)

5. *Poule* HEN

women are fragile
on dating apps
and difficult to monetise
(he said) their golden
eggs in a basket

6. *Bette* CHARD

your stem a streak
of golden red on green
(with this resilience
you're holding on) holds out
against the cuts

7. *Bouleau* BIRCH

here's a silver skin
that peels away in layers
against the pull of work
(hold tomorrow still while I
rip yesterday from your back)

8. *Jonquille* DAFFODIL

in the rushes (running late
on screens of inward eyes)
this is yellow still
trumpeting its own face
multiplied

9. *Aulne* Alder

roundish leaves
waved and toothed
in late green days
(your underwater wood
keeps the city afloat)

10. *Couvoir* Hatchery

counting the days
or counting the chickens
there you go hatching tomorrows
(where profit is nothing but
your own broken shell)

11. *Pervenche* Periwinkle

blue fetters blue
in ground cover
inching over nothing but
its own shadow (inside shell
a broken sky)

12. *Charme* Hornbeam

iron wood blunts every
blade that works it
while the slightest wind
turns up the hidden moonside
(charms your leaves to silver)

13. *Morille* MOREL

filigree holds air in the hollows
pushed out of earth
still hidden
but easy as breathing
(never work)

14. *Hêtre* BEECH

everything seems to be
hollowed out and falling
apart or is it
falling together
(tenderly encased)

15. *Abeille* BEE

reduced to function
workers suck sugar from brioche
how to speak of hive
together without queen
(this is what stung you)

16. *Laitue* LETTUCE

why oh why are we sleeping
suck this leaf with its milky juice
and sleep is an arrow
(falling more slowly)
shot into the future

17. *Mélèze* LARCH

first you don't see it
larch leaning
into wind
(a necessary lie)
then you do

18. *Ciguë* HEMLOCK

a drowsy numbness
(clustered umbels hollow
stem streaked red)
laces the spring's
inaudible nightingales

19. *Radis* RADISH

the day was red
to its swollen root
(is that what you mean
by radical) I tried to speak
in this colour

20. *Ruche* HIVE

whose mind is whose
(that was my idea you
stole it) original
honey pours over
your profile

21. *Gainier*   JUDAS TREE

for profile read
outright lie
or hidden seed
(for blossom
read treason)

22. *Romaine*   ROMAINE LETTUCE

in the snap of a leaf
one system
(who said your time
was your own)
becomes another

23. *Marronnier*   HORSE CHESTNUT

an opening not
yet an opening
still varnished brown
(spring in your fingers)
stuck days

24. *Roquette*   ROCKET

the bitter leaves
turn over (as days
turn into debts)
cutting one loss
after another

25. *Pigeon* PIGEON

strutting your losses
in grey sky feathered over
this feeling of tarmac
(your agreement
is taken as read)

26. *Lilas* LILAC

an agreement of
tense and colour
blooms
(in the time
it takes to read this)

27. *Anémone* ANEMONE

any money's
made of blood or
terminal bloom
gone with a change of wind
(branching inflorescence)

28. *Pensée* PANSY

thought flickers
behind a terminal
like the cost of your attention
gone branching
(blood flow)

29. *Myrtille* Bilberry

the promise of so much spilled
ink staining fingers tongue
hands when a flickering
thought would have been
(almost) enough

30. *Greffoir* Grafting Knife

enough that the blade
lifts bark from pith
levers the split
trims the scion (if it takes
this is what it takes)

Floréal

1. *Rose* ROSE

here is the rose here dance!
            now colour bleeds across
your money where your mouth
opens on petal after petal
useless in the bloom and buzz

2. *Chêne* OAK

permanent revolution!
            so many growth rings
written over ownership
by strength in promiscuous wind
the pollen's wild fusion

3. *Fougère* FERN

unfurl your head!
            if this feathered edge holds true
in the forest it holds
at every scale a constant
in wet green algorithms

4. *Aubépine* HAWTHORN

every flower is a fist!
            clenched against whatever
the sky might be about to promise
thicket and prickle resist
in bunches of no surrender

5. *Rossignol* NIGHTINGALE

until the song ends!
          in earshot but invisible
and what I'm reaching with is hope
arriving with no papers only
its chuckle and trill its precarious warble

6. *Ancolie* COLUMBINE

live free or die!
          a cluster of doves
or an eagle's claw
comes winging into spurred petals
wet paint suddenly in flower

7. *Muguet* LILY OF THE VALLEY

you have nothing to lose!
          only this green soaped scent
of a too-clean history
a page of nothing
ringing its poisonous bells

8. *Champignon* MUSHROOM

we champion the spore-bearing body!
          before you noticed it was there
in the tissue of earth in tentacular reach
it didn't break out but rose softly
from bonds from scattering

9. *Hyacinthe* Hyacinth

let a hundred flowers bloom!
      under the sky
corolla pressing down
make way for straight lines
and the scent of geometry

10. *Rateau* Rake

to work!
      what rises from the ground
might hit you in the face
another step forward in dry leaves
another step back

11. *Rhubarbe* Rhubarb

be realists
      demand the impossible!
the chatter and hum come closer
stalked by blades of crimson
you wouldn't believe

12. *Sainfoin* Sainfoin

never work!
      the bees revolve
round pink a poem revolves
around the names of dried-out plants
and wasted industry

13. *Bâton d'or* WALLFLOWER

no time to waste!
            up against the glitterball
dragged out and playing along
this shout of orange honey violet
is running rings round the system

14. *Chamerisier* DWARF HONEYSUCKLE

unfettered pleasure!
            no-one can own
these volatile compounds of a flower
swarming neurons
insects bound to swoon

15. *Ver à soie* SILKWORM

this is not a revolt!
            it's your cocoon
that's unravelling into
long skeins looping across
the spinning horizon

16. *Consoude* COMFREY

roots of all systems, unite!
            what runs underground
knits broken bones together
in a body botanic lifting
its head like a bell

17. *Pimprenelle* Burnet

the alarm clock is the day's
first humiliation!
            reset it to the opening
of an eye in a petal to a shift in light
they don't own this at least not yet

18. *Corbeille d'or* Aurinia

beneath the paving stones the beach!
            all this gold in a basket
spreads penniless under
the heaved stone the smash
of glass catching the sun

19. *Arroche* Orache

look in front of you!
            the spreading leaf
a bolt of green in spring
springing out of step
a season snatched

20. *Sarcloir* Hoe

something's happening!
            and you don't know where
it's all going to end this
reshaping of the soil digging furrows
scuffling the surface

21. *Statice* Sea Lavender

another world is possible!
       over salt marsh
neither sea nor land the wind
shimmers bluish on blush
everlasting

22. *Fritillaire* Fritillary

banning is banned!
       purple and snake leather
head bowed to no-one
what rules is invisible
air a silent vowel

23. *Bourrache* Borage

quick!
       I can't see anything from here
the day's emergency has us
in the blink of a starflower
coolly unfolding through millennia

24. *Valériane* Valerian

write everywhere!
       through herb and root say it
in mercurial flowers printed over sleep
a pattern of words of days and the spaces
between them that are not blank

25. *Carpe* CARP

seize the day!
        a fish sleeps any time
in muddy water with slight movements
a flicker of gills steadying fins the day
is what it swims in what swims in it

26. *Fusain* SPINDLE TREE

yell!
        a red shout bursts
in leaf in berry in flame
this burning a demand for everything
and everything now

27. *Civette* CHIVE

death to the tyrants!
        push on in the rushes
where hollow green holds up
the sharpest point
ready to pierce the sky

28. *Buglose* BUGLOSS

no peace!
        snake tongue blue
lies across the path
burning skin on contact
truth a sudden flower

29. *Sénévé* CHARLOCK

better to die in flames!
        run wild and hot
a streak of yellow into night
that falls and keeps falling
this is how to light the future

30. *Houlette* SHEPHERD'S STAFF

liberty equality fraternity!
        not the hooked neck
but freedom hefted in
wild tracks where I is another
line running through

Prairial

1. *Luzerne* ALFALFA

a field of vision bleeding at the edge
rolls through the season / purple
medic from the Medes or *al-fasfasah* from
elsewhere turning on the tongue / it grows
you cut it back / a nation is this haze

2. *Hémérocalle* DAYLILY

an orange blaze cuts through and dies
if you thought it was all over
it isn't / look down
where you can't see the spread of a root
system strangling earth / in pale fine threads

3. *Trèfle* WHITE CLOVER

a three-way split suspended
in a green chord hanging on
cut white / keep your measure
this elusive fourth a lucky strike
that doesn't resolve a thing

4. *Angélique* ANGELICA

stringy on the teeth or glued
in the icing / a day loops back
spindle-shaped thick and fleshy
beset with many long descending rootlets
from a green stem / cut and candied

5. *Canard* Duck

or rabbit / walks like a still
cut from yesterday /quacks
tomorrow / in petrol puddle
sheen / days running
like oil off whose back

6. *Mélisse* Lemon Balm

what oils of cut leaves could
soothe this gaping silence
humming like summer / in the screen
of night / its flickering colours
a chemical tide already in retreat

7. *Fromental* Oat Grass

a rehearsal of movements
over time / history
pulled between thumb and forefinger
for the feel of grass seed
scattering / cut / repeat

8. *Martagon* Martagon Lily

lilies in becoming
turbans / dragon lily / sultan lily
all-over exotica / cut the borders
wear tomorrow's foreignness
where you become me I you

9. *Serpolet* Wild Thyme

underfoot leaves crushed again
and hope / the scent cuts through
senses wired back in blue air
yesterday running wild / say now
as if this time might be different

10. *Faux* Scythe

here comes death stalking
the fields of summer / never
went away / cut and rewind
the same story felled
by repetition / never cut and dried

11. *Fraise* Strawberry

o strawberry moon where night
comes knocking at my window / cut /
o lyric poetry too slow too foreign
to say how this strange place
belongs to everyone in it

12. *Bétoine* Woundwort

after the cut / this salve
skin layers and peels / a fingernail
pushed back into place as if the body
politic grew back from a matrix
at the base of a broken fist

13. *Pois* PEA

don't let tomorrow hollow out
today's green shell
where what grows must grow
from itself / cut the repetitions
now is now is now

14. *Acacia* ACACIA

here's a single thorn in the
shape of an I / gummed with honey
I / is an alien species
cut back
the will of the people clickbait

15. *Caille* QUAIL

in the quailing heart
a door opens and a flock of birds
rushes into wind / scrappy
hopes clenched in their beaks / cut /
all this happens in a poem

16. *Oeillet* CARNATION

red blooms in muzzles of rifles
but it's bad luck this unblinking
eye of a cheap bouquet
an easy goodbye / your rights
cut like flowers

17. *Sureau* ELDER

champagne buds uncurling / almost
themselves like phrases in a second
language from this angle /cut /
or movement extending
through days without division

18. *Pavot* POPPY

don't you see this gash running
through years undercut by
violence / change was already
dropping petals / rattling
its dry seeds

19. *Tilleul* LINDEN

yellow dust in the mouth
another trashed economy
a taste of wind / cut / summer
falling in the same place /stars
crushed on the pavement

20. *Fourche* PITCHFORK

take whatever you have to hand
to lift away loose matter / cut /
slide the tines under lies and despair
and if you thought the enemy's tools might be
more specialised / well think again

21. *Barbeau* CORNFLOWER

a bolt of bloom exploding on the other side
of the forest / a denim shirt raised
as a flag changes nothing / everything
flares cobalt in a gas flame / cut /
so far away this blue

22. *Camomille* CAMOMILE

sometimes in your dream you wake up
and there isn't an infusion of anything
to calm this state / it isn't yours /
someone's close in the cut night
bleached across a Kodacolor lawn

23. *Chèvrefeuille* HONEYSUCKLE

a fresh salt wind and nectar
laces the air / goat leaf
bound around a trunk / this
stubborn winding cuts through / just
hold on long enough

24. *Caille-lait* BEDSTRAW

an acid infusion to heal
all cuts and inward wounds
curdle milk / turn cloth to gold
you made your own bed / you're lying
in it now / it's time to get up

25. *Tanche* TENCH

in slow-moving water the doctor fish
slips unnoticed from the grasp
of night / the river
cuts its losses / exporting
itself in endless departure

26. *Jasmin* JASMINE

whiteness multiplied by white
lost in its own heady scent / blind
flower of mothers and nations
who knew how the air / the air
would be cut / would cut us

27. *Verveine* VERBENA

a distant planet pulling its weight
in lemon-scented leaves
whose garden is the garden of love
cut that / right here
the weight in my chest as borders realign

28. *Thym* THYME

music comes next and the wind
in the mint and thyme / grey songs
sent out to sea / never to return
nuance the day that's already written /cut /
write it this way instead

29. *Pivoine* PEONY

I'd like to exchange this wind
for your shadows this debt
for your glamour / the cut
of your jib for the deepest purple
seeping into daylight

30. *Chariot* HANDCART

such a weight to pull through
this golden morning / as pollen
drifts where it must / cut
movement of bodies / thought /
the day goes to hell in a

96

Messidor

1. *Seigle* RYE

happens in green
in stalks that yellow
and darken to black bread
"every mouth is a history"
but can't taste its own speech

2. *Avoine* OAT

erupts in the space
of repeated sowing
full of days and days
"if you're doing time
don't expect porridge"

3. *Oignon* ONION

unravels in paper and
tears no tears
in the surface where
the skins rub "fingers
at the tip of my words"

4. *Véronique* SPEEDWELL

flashes past the corner
the eye stopped
on international blue
"not the pigment
but what binds it"

5. *Mulet* MULE

kicks off in "hybrid
vigour" in these bloodlines
that are never linear
but massed kinship tangled
and running on the hoof

6. *Romarin* ROSEMARY

grows tidal over "remember
me" before you can finish
forgetting the dead
weight of time without history
to break it and begin again

7. *Concombre* CUCUMBER

holds water in leaking
arcs of memory over
the snap of scented
hothouse "who'll spend
those green coins on your eyes"

8. *Échalote* SHALLOT

rolls like loose change
for what it's worth
a sliced pearl still
bubbling "just a matter
of when" before the crash

9. *Absinthe* WORMWOOD

speaks bitter on the tongue
before days enter in words
their taste telling you
"wormwood and sugar-plums
are not the same thing"

10. *Faucille* SICKLE

slashes through hay like
"the end" except
this time it's only
a breath between
stalk blade crackle dust

11. *Coriandre* CORIANDER

drifts citrus feathered green
the spice route ground down
to crushed bedbug nut spice "under
the pillow before sunrise" gets you
drunk on dizzy corn small change

12. *Artichaut* ARTICHOKE

peels off with the idea
you can't eat at the core
flesh stuck to the teeth
you wrap around
"an edible heart"

13. *Giroflée* GILLYFLOWER

ruffles a memory of cloves
where pain bites down
to bring all of "you" to this
medicinal sense of a body
you'd rather be beside not in

14. *Lavande* LAVENDER

confuses blue with grey
"comes out in the wash"
hazed mauve where the scent
of a vanished room
finally explains itself

15. *Chamois* CHAMOIS

runs hell for leather
or freezes all ears and
limbs in the alarm
wincing at threat where
"silent" landscapes vibrate

16. *Tabac* TOBACCO

goes up in smoke across
the screen the smell of
television gone leaving
an attitude in black and white
"you can't say that" but you did

17. *Groseille* CURRANT

bursts open on the tongue
a sour rush of juice
a stained beak singing
the same refrain "but
differently this time"

18. *Gesse* VETCHLING

signals to bee in
yellow noise a weather
headache bearing down
on this "tomorrow"
whenever that might be

19. *Cerise* CHERRY

has its time yes short
and bloody but alive
we gather in our dreams
red dress drops of coral
"the heart an open wound"

20. *Parc* PARK

merges with bodies
paths and boxy chestnuts
in the air passing where
"all that is solid" doesn't melt
you move with it

21. *Menthe* MINT

fades in pop as a love song
cutting the incense with
"nothing to lose" oh but
now you're lying who
cares the day freshens

22. *Cumin* CUMIN

edges to musty earth in
base notes the seeds
browned in oil rise into sun
the hot road winding where
"chickens and lovers won't stray"

23. *Haricot* HARICOT BEAN

empties its pockets not a bean
left from the harried land
but "ayacotli" rattles
on the tongue from Aztec
in the long slow stew

24. *Orcanète* ALKANET

dyes the people red
from its root "tenacious
flower" coarse narrow leaves
point up to sky blue
eyes bloom in spirals

25. *Pintade* Guinea Fowl

grubs and pecks at
miniature lives the last
sad bird of "summer"
spotted in savannahs of a
season somewhere else

26. *Sauge* Sage

pushes soft grey
ears into air
"once bitten twice"
the medicinal tang
cold on the lip

27. *Ail* Garlic

blooms white
breathes up close
"these mingled bodies"
decomposing
in a scale from air to earth

28. *Vesce* Vetch

flowers in the place of a word
a longing not for plants but
their names filling the mouth
with the itch of lost knowledge
or the scratch of "vetch"

29. *Blé* WHEAT

lengthens in the queue of days
but don't forget whose minutes
"matter most" in the non-stop
amnesia milling itself to dust
before the split second ripens

30. *Chalémie* SHAWM

hums with the lights on
time never switches off
but who owns this "con-
tinuous now" just pierce it
with your breath this note

Thermidor

1. *Épeautre* SPELT

day, your rough husks
run through the hours
I can count on my fingers
held up by bones
weighed in bread and stars

2. *Bouillon blanc* COMMON MULLEIN

day, your yellow spikes
reach up into the sun
jabbing at death
which is slowly revolving
around you

3. *Melon* MELON

day, you're sliced
into so many pieces
I'm all cut up and
the sugar's running
out of my grin

4. *Ivraie* RYEGRASS

day, you don't know
how to keep the grain
from grass
the mountain
from the mole

5. *Bélier* RAM

day, you keep
slamming your head
against tomorrow
as if you could
possibly win

6. *Prêle* HORSETAIL

day, you've already
disappeared leaving only
the flick of a rat's tail
vanishing
feathered green

7. *Armoise* MUGWORT

day, you just grew
there in the car park
where I didn't even
feel you brushing by
pinnate and sessile

8. *Carthame* SAFFLOWER

day, you turn
in a yellow blaze
leaving your crushed
seeds and oil
dripping in flames

9. *Mûre* BLACKBERRY

day, your black juice
bursts open
I'm caught
by the tiniest needles
snagging at the surface

10. *Arrosoir* WATERING CAN

day, you hold water
just long enough
for a thought
to unfurl in a
single shaking leaf

11. *Panic* PANIC GRASS

day, you're so wound up
a swollen thread
try to let go
like grass all flesh
flung wide

12. *Salicorne* GLASSWORT

day, your body
sucks up salt and moisture
green against the odds
resisting
footsteps teeth

13. *Abricot*   APRICOT

day, here's the sunset already
mish mish
precocious fruit
blink and
you'll

14. *Basilic*   BASIL

day, your kingliness
is next to comedy
Brush or Fawlty
monstrous little monarchs
crushed leaves

15. *Brebis*   EWE

day, here you go again
in sour milk and lanolin
trampling tomorrow's grass
with your cloven hooves
and wild yellow eyes

16. *Guimauve*   MARSHMALLOW

day, don't sugar
the root of survival
your resilience
tensed against
the damage

17. *Lin* FLAX

day, you fold over
like clean sheets
at the beginning
then rumpled
by possession as a stain

18. *Amande* ALMOND

day, summer's
sweet kernel
your eye
falls on us
like a sledgehammer

19. *Gentiane* GENTIAN

day, you blink out
wildest habitat
difficult Illyrian
flower bitter blue
what eyes

20. *Écluse* LOCK

day, you began
with such level calm
then dropped as pressure
built behind the gates
where tomorrow foams

21. *Carline* Silver Thistle

day, when everything needles
you have to grasp the stem
where the aureole is
still just about
holding up

22. *Caprier* Caper

day, you're a burst
of sharpness on the tongue
you make me want to taste
the trees asphalt rocks mud sand
that blurred mass on the horizon

23. *Lentille* Lentil

day, you're just a lost
contact lens glinting
out of sight I didn't
notice the world
turning through you

24. *Aunée* Elecampane

day, these tears
that launched
a thousand faces
are sailing adrift
in a hospital corridor

25. *Loutre* OTTER

day, I didn't see you
slip under the surface
or your sleek head rise
with a fish
between your teeth

26. *Myrte* MYRTLE

day, you grow
from planted sprigs
the woody stem
and not the flower
dividing as love is division

27. *Colza* RAPESEED

day, I'll pour you
over choppy sea
to smooth it flat
as electric yellow fields
pulsing under grey

28. *Lupin* LUPIN

day, you whorl around
an upward movement
in your skyscraper petals
already falling
come back

29. *Coton* COTTON

day, you're gone in a cloud
where the price of labour
spun out over oceans
broken backs
snaps tight

30. *Moulin* MILL

day, it's back to the grind
where hoarded grain
tips to rioting point
as a calendar's weight
revolves on bread

Fructidor

1. *Prune* PLUM

its skin is a bruise coming late again
where slow time slips between
branches through the fingers
of the dead and into this future
that can't stop imagining itself.

2. *Millet* MILLET

in the season that hasn't yet arrived
you're nothing but a dot in the distance
unconvincing as a packet of seeds
or a stranger you don't see coming
and don't want to trust with your life.

3. *Licoperde* PUFFBALL

suddenly skull-size to put it baldly
I didn't recognise you. or I didn't
recognise *I* stranded and mycelic
ready to grasp the day
then vanish in a puff of spores.

4. *Éscourgeon* SIX-ROW BARLEY

we pulled it through our fingers
where the brittle spike snapped off
and rubbed the husks away. hand
to mouth. I'm writing grain
by grain for you I can't see.

5. *Saumon* SALMON

return upstream though it wasn't
the same river even the first
time round. start again become
finned and salt. I'm invisible
from where you are now.

6. *Tubéreuse* TUBEROSE

between water and daylight catch
the scent of darkness as unstoppered
feeling swollen at the root. I'd say
it was mine if this body wouldn't
burst at so much coincidence.

7. *Sucrion* NAKED BARLEY

how can anyone remember the taste
of common good when even the word
for it has all but disappeared
like this this floury and productive grain
esteemed in several provinces.

8. *Apocyn* DOGBANE

will regulate the beating of the heart
or steady thump of days whether it's
the plant or its name that keeps blood
pulsing through the herbal in its
spell of synchronous movement.

9. *Réglisse* LIQUORICE

there's nothing to chew on but words
now the sweetness has gone
from being outside looking in
and there's a darkness in your throat
that you can't swallow.

10. *Échelle* LADDER

time to step up. stop. don't
stop. between one rung and
another there's a shift of scale
a tilt in the horizon that hasn't
yet come any closer.

11. *Pastèque* WATERMELON

I am the fruit of your dreams. desire
split open in the horror soundtrack
is where the seeds are. gouge
a beginning from the rolling credits
this time with more feeling.

12. *Fenouil* FENNEL

peel off strung layers to the green core
curled and fronded. listen up. even if
it's always too late and the last time
around never quite worked the stopped
season isn't dead but waiting.

13. *Épine-vinette* Barberry

summer plays on repeat. push to
the limits of a surface and break.
burst into fruit and then fall full
stop. but do this so often that stopping
is a way of stepping through.

14. *Noix* Walnut

hidden in its own boat a curled ear
listens for the noise of drowning.
stop there and wait it out between times
as summer moves on the same
summer beginning somewhere else.

15. *Truite* Trout

tickled mud moves in the shallows
dappled silver black. what's
disappearing with nothing but a blip
of air on the surface is just the air
still on the surface of a day.

16. *Citron* Lemon

windows of sliced yellow open on a scene
you thought you'd forgotten but which is
still replaying with ice and sharp sun perhaps
no lemon after all and since that's you
you're watching this is not a memory.

17. *Cardière* TEASEL

teased and carded every knot
unlocks its fibres ready to be spun
the length of a wheel turning
a looped strand of work or time
stretching in the tendons of a hand.

18. *Nerprun* BUCKTHORN

ink seed blackens the page where
the words are not yet out of the woods.
that's you smudged in the spaces
where you're trying to escape
from these strata of genes and calendars.

19. *Tagète* MEXICAN MARIGOLD

show me the way to yellow fields
where the sun comes down and flattens
time into blocks of colour moving
on the eye. a hard enough stare turns
day into day's afterimage. aftershock.

20. *Hotte* CONICAL BASKET

as if recalling all these names and their
shaky translations would weave time
into twisted wicker. as if weaving time
could make it portable. as if the days
of a calendar would carry us through.

21. *Églantier* DOG ROSE

late sun pricks the first red fruit.
you're bleeding all over this flushed
season where the boundary isn't
skin but a membrane separating
now from what comes next.

22. *Noisette* HAZELNUT

on the twig three wishes. in a nutshell each one
cracks open releasing a garment woven from
pure desire which at the blink of an owl
will dress you in green in dawn in white
for the forest the dance the ever-after horses.

23. *Houblon* HOP

change dreams. go back to sleep and
unravel the bristling stems of who or
what you thought you might become
when circadian rhythms roused you
in this spiral clockwise and up.

24. *Sorgho* SORGHUM

if it all boils down to bread or letting them
eat or having one's cake and eating it
here is a mouth and here is grain
and here is the word for it passing
from your mouth to mine.

25. *Écrevisse* CRAYFISH

take a body's ability to feel pain
divided into twenty segments. stop.
articulate your feeling here and there
and in this and in that other
who isn't inside your shell.

26. *Bigarade* SEVILLE ORANGE

why not be a painter when one thing
after another enters your field of vision
going rapidly out of date as the temperature
rises to an orange so bitter you can
no longer see or taste the word for it.

27. *Verge d'or* GOLDEN ROD

yellow becomes its own gold reflected
in multiple touchscreens. who knows
what it's worth the tracking from eye to
flower complicit in sunlight or data
as outline of a day that isn't yours.

28. *Maïs* CORN

unfold the crinkled leaf and peel it
back from all the starch and sweetness
anyone could need then join the dots
with suns going round and round
dizzily enough times to make a life.

29. *Marron* LARGE CHESTNUT

there's no way to sugar over this globe
with its split shell and crevices. a planet
turns in time with scratches on the record
going back to the beginning again.
but we haven't even been here once.

30. *Panier* BASKET

its circumference is the length
of a revolution that doesn't stop
here. hold on to the heaped up day
you'll never reach around however
far you stretch out your arms.

Notes

After an early prototype devised by Sylvain Maréchal in 1788, Gilbert Romme led a commission to develop the French Republican Calendar that was in use from 1793 and dated from the birth of the Republic on September 22nd 1792. This sequence of poems draws particularly on the contribution of Fabre d'Églantine, who composed the names of the months and suggested naming the days after plants, animals and objects that were significant to the rural economy. The metric organisation of ten-day weeks, *décades*, is not reproduced here, although it can be seen in the pattern of dedications of every tenth day to an agricultural implement and every fifth day to an animal. For historical and political context see Sanja Perovic, *The Calendar in Revolutionary France: Perceptions of Time in Literature, Culture, Politics*, Cambridge University Press, 2012.

The Republican Calendar for Year II, 22nd September 1793, can be found at BnF Gallica: https://gallica.bnf.fr/ark:/12148/btv1b10547000p

p. 12 'POTIRON *Squash*' and 'BELLE DE NUIT *Marvel of Peru*' refer to the *I Ching* or *Book of Changes*, translated by Richard Wilhelm and Cary F. Baynes, 1951, from which Pink Floyd's 'Chapter 24' on *The Piper at the Gates of Dawn*, 1967, is derived. See also Arthur Lee's 'She Comes in Colors' by Love, 1966.

p. 14 '*Navet* TURNIP' refers to John Ashbery's 'Farm Implements and Rutabagas in a Landscape', 1966.

p. 15 'Endless Summer' was a genetically engineered tomato introduced and withdrawn in the 1990s.

p. 23 '*Dentelaire* LEADWORT' refers to Karl Marx, *Eighteenth Brumaire of Louis Bonaparte*, 1852.

p. 40 '*Fumier* MANURE' refers to the title of Half Man Half Biscuit's song 'National Shite Day' from *CSI: Ambleside*, 2008.

p. 55 '*Lièvre* HARE' quotes Charles F. Partington, editor, *The British Cyclopaedia of the Arts, Sciences, History, Geography, Literature, Natural History, and Biography*, 1838.

— 'Guède WOAD' includes phrases from William Hope-Jones, 'National Anthem of the Ancient Britons' in *The Hackney Scout Song Book*, 1921.

p. 56 '*Chélidoine* CELANDINE' quotes John Gerard, *The Herball or Generall Historie of Plantes*, 1597.

p. 61 '*Bêche* SPADE' refers to Ian Hamilton Finlay's 'Ventose' and 'Osez', bronze and stone (with Jamie Sargeant), 1991, Tate Collection.

p. 64 '*Mandragore* MANDRAKE' mentions practices noted by Pierre le Brun and Jean-Baptiste Thiers in *Superstitions Anciennes et Modernes, prejugés vulgaires qui ont induit les peuples à des usages & à des pratiques contraires à la religion*, 1733.

— '*Persil* PARSLEY' has in mind Caroline Bergvall's series of installations, *Say: 'Parsley'*, 2001 onwards.

p. 79 '*Rose* ROSE' quotes Marx, *Eighteenth Brumaire of Louis Bonaparte*.

p. 94 '*Caille-lait* BEDSTRAW' draws on Nicholas Culpeper, *The Complete Herbal*, 1653.

p. 101 '*Absinthe* WORMWOOD' quotes John Locke, *An Essay Concerning Human Understanding*, 1689.

p. 103 '*Cerise* CHERRY' references Jean-Baptiste Clément's song, 'Le temps des cerises', 1866.

— '*Parc* PARK' quotes Friedrich Engels and Karl Marx, *The Communist Manifesto*, 1848.

p. 112 '*Abricot* APRICOT' refers to the Arabic word for this fruit. It figures in a dismissive colloquial response to wishful thinking about the future, *filmishmish*, which is roughly equivalent to 'dream on'.